DASH DIET BREAKFAST RECIPES

Energize Your Mornings with Nutritious and Delicious Breakfasts on the DASH Diet (2023 Guide for Beginners)

Hattie Daniel

Introduction

The DASH diet, or Dietary Approaches to Stop Hypertension, is one of the most well-known and highly regarded dietary regimens.

ways to enhance health. The DASH diet, known for its solid nutritional base, was initially designed to help individuals with high blood pressure or at risk of hypertension naturally decrease their levels and live a better lifestyle. The DASH diet, which is widely acclaimed in the health and fitness sectors, quickly became so well known for its excellent outcomes that others started adopting it to lose weight and minimize the consequences of chronic illness, such as inflammation and diabetes, in their lives. As you will see, when you concentrate on natural foods that are high in vitamins and minerals, your body starts to repair itself.

You may be eating DASH because your doctor advised you to, you may be seeking the healthiest approach to shedding those excess pounds, or you may have realized that it is time to respect your body by providing it with the nourishment it requires.

Whatever led you here, you are about to learn how delightful eating according to the DASH diet can be. Breakfast is often regarded as the most essential meal of the day. It's the starting line, and how you take off from there will decide how far you go in the race. Too often, we begin our days with merely coffee or a drive-through meal that does little to fuel our bodies. Most people have hectic mornings, and the prospect of having the time to prepare and eat something nutritious and substantial may be overwhelming. The purpose of this book is to present you with new and unique breakfast dishes that will appeal to your taste buds, lifestyle, and hectic schedule. You'll discover DASH-friendly meals to fit your morning routine, whether it's a quiet weekend morning or a grab-and-go morning when you need to get out the door quickly. One thing to remember is that many of these dishes may be made ahead of time, saving you even more time in the mornings.

Why is DASH used?

You'll note that the recipes in this book mostly use fresh, unprocessed ingredients. The DASH diet's key concepts are to eat foods that are low in fat, low in sodium, and rich in particular nutrients like calcium, magnesium, and potassium. DASH's effectiveness stems from its mix of dietary methods. The bulk of the things you consume throughout the day are grains, vegetables, and fruits. Protein, iron, and calcium are all provided by lean protein sources and low-fat dairy in acceptable proportions. Because the DASH diet's main goal was to treat hypertension, it is naturally low in salt. The appropriate daily salt intake for most individuals is between 1500 and 2300 mg, depending on their dietary demands and concerns. Keep in mind that these are upper limits, and aiming for lower numbers is a fantastic objective. However, it is critical to keep sodium in context. Our bodies need salt; we've simply gotten into the habit of eating too much of it. It is difficult to completely remove salt from the body; instead, the DASH diet promotes a healthy awareness of sodium intake. Sodium may be found in healthy foods such as reduced-fat dairy and professionally prepared whole grain breads. By consuming these items in moderation, you are unlikely to surpass the recommended limits. Eating highly processed meals that employ salt as a preservative and flavoring ingredient may be detrimental to sodium levels. One teaspoon of salt exceeds the top limit of permissible sodium content. Many of us liberally sprinkle salt on our meals without realizing how much we are really adding. Instead of salt, these DASH recipes encourage you to concentrate on natural tastes and seasonings using fresh and   dried   herbs.

Perhaps you choose DASH not because you are worried about your blood pressure but because you want to lose weight. You may believe that salt restrictions do not apply to you; nonetheless, lowering sodium and boosting potassium can help you lose weight and reduce bloating quickly   and   efficiently.

Nothing beats a DASH-friendly breakfast to get your day started. The tastes here are appealing to a broad range of people, so you can confidently share them with your family and friends, knowing that each dish contains complete nutrition from fresh, healthy ingredients.

Grains

A fantastic breakfast staple is the correct grain, served just so. The good news is that you don't have to limit yourself to boring, plain oatmeal or bran flakes. When it comes to healthful and tasty breakfast foods, grains may take on a variety of personalities. Throw off your preconceived notions and embrace these delectable, healthful, and one-of-a-kind breakfast alternatives.

Buckwheat Pancakes: 2

Ingredients

2 tablespoons sugar or chosen sugar alternative
1 cup buckwheat flour
1 tsp. baking powder
1 tsp. baking soda
1/4 cups fat-free buttermilk
1 large egg
1/2 teaspoons pure vanilla or almond essence
1 teaspoon lemon zest
Optional garnish: fresh fruit
Cooking spray made with vegetable oil

Directions

1. In a mixing bowl, combine the flour, sugar or sugar substitute, baking powder, and baking soda. Whisk to combine.
2. In a separate dish, whisk together the buttermilk, egg, almond or vanilla essence, and lemon zest. Mix well with a whisk.
3. Mix the wet and dry ingredients just until they are combined.
4. Heat a nonstick skillet over medium-low heat with cooking spray.
5. Pour about 14 cups of the batter into the skillet and cook until bubbles form on the top, about 3 minutes.
6. Flip and cook for another 2 minutes.
7. If wanted, serve immediately with fresh fruit.

Information on Nutrition

Sodium 440.2 mg, potassium 532.9 mg, total carbs 42.8 g, dietary fiber 9.1 g, sugars 13.3 g, protein 15.8 g

Power Protein Waffles, Portion 2

Ingredients

1/4 cups crushed flax meal
1 cup whole wheat flour
1/2 cup oats
3 eggs
1 cup plain nonfat yogurt
1 teaspoon of orange juice
1/2 teaspoons pure vanilla extract
1/2 teaspoons ground cinnamon
3/4 cup skim milk

Directions

1. Preheat the waffle maker.
2. Combine the whole wheat flour, flax meal, and oatmeal in a mixing bowl.
3. Whisk the eggs in a separate bowl before adding the yogurt, orange juice, vanilla essence, and cinnamon. Blend well.
4. Combine the dry components with the liquid ingredients, mixing as little as possible.
5. Stir in the milk until a thick but pourable batter forms.
6. Pour into the waffle iron and cook according to the manufacturer's directions.

Information on Nutrition

Sodium 231.2 mg,
potassium 607.2 mg,
total carbs 76.0 g,
dietary fiber 12.3 g,
sugars 15.6 g,
protein 31.9 g

Muffins with Whole Grain and Dried Fruit
Serves 12

Ingredients

1/2 cups whole grain flour
2 tbsp. baking powder
1/2 teaspoons ground cinnamon
1/4 tsp ground nutmeg
1/4 teaspoons of ginger powder
2 eggs
1 tablespoon honey (or sugar alternative of choice)
1 teaspoon vanilla essence, pure
1/4 cups liquefied coconut oil

1/2 cups apple juice, unsweetened
1/4 cups of orange juice
1/4 cup chopped dates
1/4 cups cranberries, dry
1/4 cups chopped dried apricots
1/2 cups chopped, unsalted pistachios

Directions

1. Preheat the oven to 400 degrees Fahrenheit and prepare 12 muffin cups with paper liners.
2. Combine the whole wheat flour, baking powder, cinnamon, nutmeg, and ginger in a mixing bowl.
3. Lightly whisk the eggs in a separate dish before adding the honey, vanilla extract, coconut oil, apple juice, and orange juice.
4. Combine the wet and dry ingredients, mixing just until combined. The mixture will most likely be lumpy. Make sure not to overmix.
5. Combine the dates, cranberries, apricots, and pistachios in a mixing bowl.
6. Fill muffin pans about 3/4 full.
7. Bake for 12–15 minutes, or until a toothpick inserted into the middle comes out clean.

Information on Nutrition

Total fat: 7.9 g, saturated fat: 4.5 g, sodium: 94.0 mg, potassium: 147.8 mg, total carbs: 23.3 g, dietary fiber: 3.0 g, sugars: 6.3 g, protein: 4.3 g

Overnight Berry Stuffed French Toast

Ingredients

8 slices whole wheat bread, thick
6 beaten eggs
4 cups of milk with a reduced fat content
1 teaspoon vanilla essence, pure
1 teaspoon ground cinnamon
1 teaspoon ground nutmeg
2 tbsp. lemon zest
34 cups cubed low-fat cream cheese
12 cup blueberries, fresh
12 cups chopped fresh strawberries

Directions

1. Combine the eggs, milk, vanilla essence, cinnamon, nutmeg, and lemon zest in a mixing dish. Place aside.
2. Place four slices of bread in an 8-by-8 baking dish.
3. Spread cubed cream cheese, blueberries, and strawberries on top of each slice.
4. Top each with an extra slice of bread.
5. Pour the custard mixture over the bread in the baking dish, covering as much as possible.
6. Place in the refrigerator overnight, covered.
Preheat the oven to 350°F.
8. Bake for 30 minutes, covered with aluminum foil.
9. Remove the lid and continue baking for another 20 minutes, or until the toast is golden brown.

Information on Nutrition

Sodium 564.1 mg, potassium 609.9 mg, total carbs 42.0 g, dietary fiber 4.9 g, sugars 17.9 g, protein 30.8 g

4 Individual Whole Wheat Puff Pancakes

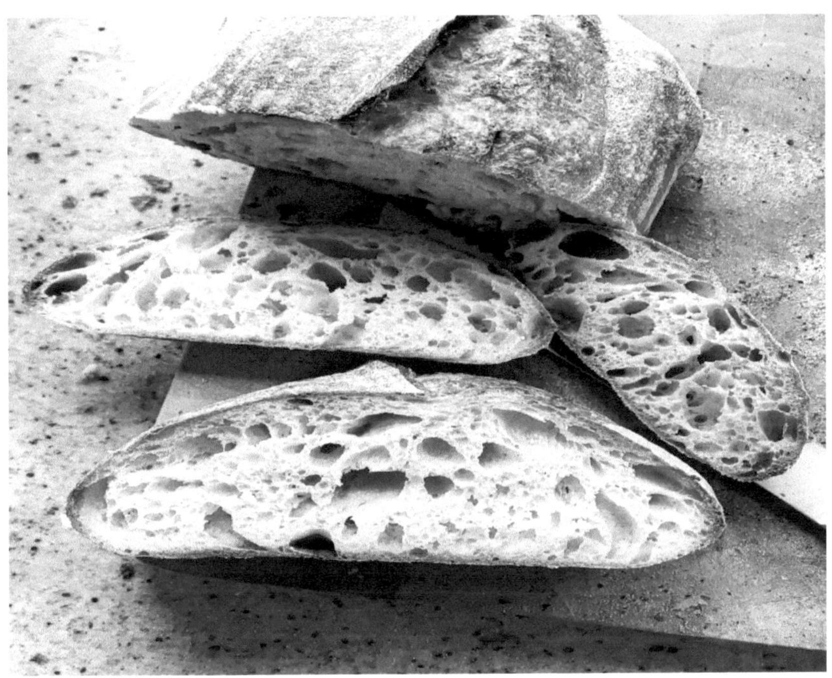

Ingredients

6 beaten eggs
1 cup skim milk
1 teaspoon vanilla essence, pure
1 cup whole grain flour
12 teaspoons of ginger powder
1 cup sliced fresh peaches
12 cup blueberries, fresh
Cooking spray or oil

Directions

1. Preheat the oven to 425°F and gently coat six individual

ramekins with cooking spray.
2. Whisk together the eggs, milk, vanilla essence, wheat flour, and crushed ginger until well combined.
3. Divide the mixture among the ramekins and top with the peaches and blueberries.
4. Place the ramekins on a baking sheet and bake for 20 minutes.
5. Bake for 25–30 minutes, or until golden brown and the middle is firm.

Information on Nutrition

258.7 calories,
7.9 g total fat,
 2.5 g saturated fat,
133.3 mg sodium,
298.9 mg potassium,
32.9 g total carbs,
5.0 g dietary fiber,
9.2 g sugars,
15.9 g protein

Fruit Baked Oatmeal Makes 4-6 Servings

Ingredients

1 cup chopped apple
1 cup blueberries, fresh
1 cup chopped fresh blackberries
2 cups oats, rolled
1/2 cups chopped walnuts
1 tsp. baking powder
1 teaspoon ground cinnamon
1 cup skim milk
1/2 cups plain low-fat yogurt
1 teaspoon vanilla extract
2 tbsp. honey (or sugar alternative of choice)
1 egg and 1 egg yolk

Directions

1. Preheat the oven to 375°F and gently grease an 8-by-8 baking dish.
2. Combine the apples, blueberries, blackberries, oats, walnuts, baking powder, and cinnamon in a mixing dish.
3. In a separate dish, whisk together the milk, yogurt, vanilla extract, honey, and egg. Whisk until smooth.
4. Combine the fruit and grains with the liquid mixture. Combine thoroughly.
5. Transfer to a baking tray and bake for 30 minutes.
6. Bake at 350°F for 45–50 minutes.
7. Allow it to cool slightly before slicing into squares to serve.

Information on Nutrition

Sodium 191.8 mg,
potassium 397.1 mg,
total carbs 57.5 g,
dietary fiber 8.7 g,
sugars 24.9 g,
protein 13.8 g

Carrot Spice Overnight Oats 4

Ingredients

2 cups oats, old-fashioned
1 cup shredded carrots
2 tbsp shredded unsweetened coconut
1/4 cups chopped walnuts
1/4 cups dried apricots
1/2 teaspoons pure vanilla essence
2 cups unsweetened coconut milk or reduced-fat milk

Directions

1. Combine the oats, carrots, coconut, walnuts, and dried

apricots in a mixing dish. Toss to combine.
2. Whisk together the vanilla essence and the milk.
3. Place the oat mixture in a mason jar or other container
with a cover.
Pour the milk over it and carefully cover.
4. Refrigerate for at least 12 hours or overnight. Refrigerate
immediately or reheat in the microwave for 1-2 minutes.

Information on Nutrition

274.7 calories,
Sodium 71.7 mg,
potassium 342.5 mg,
total carbs 39.1 g,
dietary fiber 5.8 g,
sugars 10.3 g,
protein 10.8 g

Sweet Rosemary Oats

Ingredients

2 cups oats, old-fashioned
1/2 cups chopped walnuts
2 tbsp. chopped fresh rosemary
1 teaspoon pink peppercorns, ground
2 cups skim milk
1 tablespoon honey (or sugar alternative of choice)
Optional fresh strawberries for serving

Directions

1. In a mixing bowl, combine the oats, walnuts, rosemary, and pink pepper. Toss to combine and transfer to a mason jar or other covered container.
2. Mix the milk and honey together and pour over the oat mixture.
3. Refrigerate for 12 hours or overnight, covered.
4. Warm in the microwave for 1–2 minutes before serving.
5. If preferred, garnish with fresh strawberries.

Information on Nutrition

305.3 calories,
13.1 g total fat,
1.0 g saturated fat,
52.0 mg sodium,
259.9 mg potassium,
39.5 g total carbs,
5.0 g dietary fiber,
11.9 g sugars, and 11.4 g protein.

Warming Spicy Quinoa

Ingredients

2 cups coconut milk, unsweetened
1 teaspoon ground cinnamon
1/2 teaspoons of ginger powder
quarter teaspoon cardamom
1/8 teaspoons cilantro
1/2 teaspoons pure vanilla extract
1 tablespoon honey (or sugar alternative of choice)
1 cup quinoa, uncooked
If desired, garnish with Qalnuts.

Directions

1. Combine the coconut milk, cinnamon, ginger, cardamom, coriander, vanilla essence, and honey (or sugar alternative) in a saucepan.
2. Cook over medium heat until the liquid starts to boil.
3. Stir in the quinoa. Reduce heat to low, cover, and let simmer for 15-20 minutes, or until liquid is largely absorbed and grain is soft.
4. If preferred, serve warm with walnuts.

Information on Nutrition

389.4 calories, 24.0 g total fat, 18.2 g saturated fat, 31.4 mg sodium, 0.9 mg potassium, 37.0 g total carbs, 3.0 g dietary fiber, 5.9 g sugars, 7.5 g protein

Chocolate Covered Banana Quinoa: 4 server

Ingredients

2 cups unsweetened almond milk or reduced-fat milk
2 tbsp. dark cocoa powder
1 tablespoon honey or sugar alternative of choice
1 cup quinoa, uncooked
14 cups dark chocolate shavings (optional) 1 cup sliced
bananas

Directions
1. Combine the milk or almond milk, dark chocolate

powder, and honey in a saucepan. Stir continuously over medium-high heat until the mixture bubbles.
2. Stir in the quinoa and turn the heat to low. Cover and cook for 15-20 minutes, or until most of the liquid has been absorbed and the grain is soft.
3. Garnish with sliced banana and chocolate shavings, if preferred.

Information on Nutrition

Sodium 109.2 mg,
potassium 227.0 mg,
total carbs 49.4 g,
dietary fiber 5.5 g,
sugars 15.4 g,
protein 7.4 g

Porridge with Harvest Amaranth
2 servings

Ingredients

1/2 cup amaranth
2 cups skim milk
1/2 teaspoons ground nutmeg
1/8 tsp ground cloves
1/2 cups chopped apple
1/2 cups chopped pears
1 teaspoon ground cinnamon
1 tablespoon honey or sugar alternative of choice

If desired, garnish with chopped nuts.

Directions

1. In a saucepan, bring the milk, nutmeg, and ground cloves to a boil over medium-high heat.
2. Stir in the amaranth. Cover and simmer for 20 minutes, or until the liquid has been absorbed and the grain is soft. As required, add extra water or milk while cooking.
3. Meanwhile, gently coat a sauté pan with olive oil and add the apples, pears, cinnamon, and honey. Cook, stirring constantly, until the fruit softens and some of the natural juices are released, about 5–7 minutes.
4. Remove the cover and stir in the fruit mixture after the amaranth has completed cooking.
5. Serve immediately, if preferred, garnished with nuts.

Information on Nutrition

331.2 calories,
3.3 g total fat, 1.1 g saturated fat, 113.4 mg sodium, 642.5 mg potassium, 61.4 g total carbs, 8.8 g dietary fiber, 28.8 g sugars, 15.5 g protein

2 Open-Faced Avocado Breakfast Sandwiches

Ingredients

1/2 c. goat cheese
1 tablespoon chopped sundried tomatoes
1 tablespoon chopped fresh chives
4 pieces of sprouted whole grain bread
1 medium-sized sliced tomato
1/4 cups toasted, unsalted pumpkin seeds
1 avocado, sliced
1 teaspoon black pepper, freshly ground

Directions

1. In a mixing dish, combine the goat cheese, sundried tomatoes, and chives. Blend until smooth.

2. While the bread is still warm, lightly toast it and sprinkle it with the goat cheese mixture.
3. Garnish with tomato slices, avocado slices, pumpkin seeds, and freshly ground black pepper to taste.
4. Serve right away.

Information on Nutrition

Sodium 375.8 mg,
potassium 974.6 mg,
total carbs 46.1 g,
dietary fiber 14.7 g,
sugars 2.1 g,
protein 21.6 g

Breakfast Bruschetta
Serves 4

Ingredients

6 beaten eggs
1/2 teaspoons black pepper
1 tablespoon minced fresh chives
1 tablespoon of olive oil
1/6 whole wheat baguette slices
1/2 cups skim ricotta
cheese 1/4 cups chopped fresh basil
1/4 cups chopped fresh tomatoes

1/4 cups chopped red onion

Directions

1. Heat the oven to 350°F.
2. Arrange the baguette slices on a baking sheet and gently spray with oil. Bake for 10 minutes, or until the bread is lightly toasted.
3. Combine the ricotta cheese and basil in a mixing bowl. Place aside.
4. Heat a skillet over medium heat, lightly oiling it. Combine the eggs, chives, and black pepper in a mixing bowl. Cook, scrambling with a tiny spatula, until the eggs are softly set, 3–4 minutes.
5. Spread the ricotta mixture evenly on each piece of bread.
6. Arrange eggs, basil, tomatoes, and onions on top.
7. Serve right away.

Information on Nutrition

306.5 calories,
11.8 g total fat,
4.1 g saturated fat,
146.3 mg sodium,
182.6 mg potassium,
30.6 g total carbs,
3.3 g dietary fiber,
2.4 g sugars,
19.2 g protein

Multigrain Savory Breakfast Casserole: Serves 6–8

Ingredients

8 cups cubed whole grain bread
1 tablespoon of olive oil
2 cups chopped tomatoes
2 cups asparagus spears
2 cloves of garlic, smashed and minced
1/2 cup fresh basil,
chopped 2 tablespoons fresh chives,

1/2 teaspoons black pepper
1 cup shredded low-fat white cheddar 8 eggs,
beaten 1 cup low-fat milk

Directions

1. Preheat the oven to 375°F and gently grease a 9-by-13-inch baking dish.
2. Heat the olive oil in a skillet over medium heat. Combine the tomatoes, asparagus, and garlic in a mixing bowl. Cook for 3 minutes.
3. Arrange the bread pieces in an even layer in the baking dish.
4. Top with the tomato and asparagus combination, then the basil, black pepper, and white cheddar.
5. Combine the eggs and milk in a mixing bowl. Pour the mixture into the baking dish, coating the bread pieces evenly.
6. Bake for 30-35 minutes, or until the middle is fully set, in the oven.
7. Set aside to cool somewhat before serving.

Information on Nutrition

276.9 calories,
11.8 g total fat,
3.6 g saturated fat,
365.5 mg sodium,
502.7 mg potassium,
22.8 g total carbs,
4.2 g dietary fiber,
4.6 g sugars,
20.5 g protein

Smoothies with fruits

Do you want something sweet in the morning? When you try any of these DASH-friendly, fruity breakfast dishes, your craving for unhealthy sweets will fade as you relish the ripe and bursting fresh flavors of these delights.

4 Ingredients:
Strawberry Chia Breakfast Pudding

2 cups coconut milk, unsweetened
1/2 cups chia seeds
3 cups sliced strawberries
1 teaspoon vanilla essence, pure
1 teaspoon of honey

Directions

1. In a blender, mix the coconut milk and strawberries until smooth.
2. Combine the chia seeds, vanilla essence, and honey in a mixing bowl. Stir well.
3. Refrigerate for at least 6 hours or overnight.

Information on Nutrition

314.8 calories, 25.0 g total fat, 18.2 g saturated fat, 31.6 mg sodium, 192.0 mg potassium, 22.1 g total carbs, 7.1 g dietary fiber, 11.8 g sugars, 4.5 g protein

Fruit Salad for a Sunny Morning:
4 Ingredients

2 cups diced cantaloupe
1 cup of fresh pineapple pieces
2 cups chopped apples
1 cup sliced peaches
2 cups chopped strawberries
1 cup vanilla low-fat yogurt
1 teaspoon lemon zest
1 tablespoon chopped fresh mint
If desired, garnish with sliced almonds.

Directions

1. In a large mixing bowl, combine all of the fruit. Toss to combine.
2. Combine the yogurt, lemon zest, and mint in a mixing bowl. Combine thoroughly.

3. Toss the fruit in the yogurt dressing to coat.
4. If preferred, garnish with chopped almonds.

Information on Nutrition

162.6 calories,
1.2 g total fat,
0.4 g saturated fat,
48.7 mg sodium,
320.7 mg potassium,
37.0 g total carbs,
5.1 g dietary fiber,
31.2 g sugars,
3.8 g protein

Breakfast Fruit Tart serves 8

Ingredients

2 dates cup
1/2 cups orange juice 1 cup warm water
1/2 cups walnuts, unsalted
1 cup vanilla nonfat yogurt
1/2 cups reduced-fat cream cheese
1 teaspoon lime zest
1 cup sliced kiwi
2 cups sliced fresh strawberries
1 cup blueberries, fresh
1 cup sliced fresh papaya Vegetable oil or frying spray

Directions

1. Combine the dates, water, and orange juice in a mixing dish. Allow for 10-15 minutes to allow the dates to hydrate.
2. Remove the dates from the juice and coarsely slice them.
3. In a food processor, combine the dates and walnuts and pulse until smooth.
4. Lightly oil a 9-inch pie plate and push the date-walnut mixture into it, spreading it evenly over the bottom and edges.
5. Combine the yogurt, cream cheese, and lemon zest in a mixing bowl. Blend until smooth. Fill the crust with the mixture.
6. Garnish with fresh fruit and place in the refrigerator for 2 hours.
7. Slice before serving.

Information on Nutrition

378.2 calories,
18.4 g total fat,
3.2 g saturated fat,
66.5 mg sodium,
643.4 mg potassium,
53.1 g total carbs,
7.5 g dietary fiber,
38.7 g sugars,
8.0 g protein

Fruit Salsa with Whole Wheat Pita Chips
Makes 6 Servings

Ingredients

2 cups sliced fresh strawberries
2 cups diced apples
1 cup raspberries, fresh
1 cup diced fresh pineapple
1 cup chopped fresh mango
2 tbsp. lime juice

1/4 cups sugarless peach preserves
6 whole wheat pitas, each sliced into 8 wedges
1/2 teaspoons cinnamon,
1 teaspoon olive oil

Directions

1. Heat the oven to 350°F.
2. Lightly brush the pitas with olive oil and sprinkle with cinnamon.
Place on a baking sheet in a uniform layer. Place in the oven for 10–12 minutes, or until gently brown and crisp. Remove from the oven and set aside to cool.
3. Meanwhile, put the strawberries, apples, raspberries, pineapple, and mango in a mixing dish. Toss to combine.
4. Heat the peach preserves and lime juice in a small saucepan over low heat until the preserves begin to liquefy but are not yet hot.
5. Toss the fruit with the preserves to coat.
6. Refrigerate until ready to serve with cinnamon chips, about 30 minutes.

Information on Nutrition

Sodium, 281.3 mg;
potassium, 233.0 mg;
total carbs, 44.2 g;
dietary fiber, 7.4 g;
sugars, 15.8 g;
protein, 4.8 g.

Servings of Pumpkin Smoothie

Ingredients

1/2 cups pumpkin puree
1 cup skim milk
1 cup sliced bananas
1/2 teaspoons pure vanilla extract
1/2 tsp pumpkin pie spice
2 tablespoons pure maple syrup
1 cup of ice

Directions

1. In a blender or food processor, combine all of the ingredients and mix until smooth.
2. Pour into cold glasses and serve immediately.

Information on Nutrition

Sodium 197.7 mg,
potassium 600.4 mg,

total carbs 26.3 g,
dietary fiber 2.6 g,
sugars 16.1 g,
protein 5.4 g

Smoothie with Beets and Red Velvet
Serves 2
Ingredients
2 cups raspberries, fresh
1/2 cups diced beet
1 cup orange juice, unsweetened
1/2 cups fat-free yogurt
1/4 cups chopped almonds,
1 cup ice
Directions
1. In a blender, combine all of the ingredients and mix until smooth.
2. Pour into cold glasses and serve immediately.
Information on Nutrition
243.0 calories, 7.4 g total fat, 0.9 g saturated fat, 62.8 mg sodium, 617.8 mg potassium, 40.0 g total carbs, 11.0 g dietary fiber, 21.0 g sugars, 7.4 g protein

Smoothie with Carrot Cake
Serves 2

Ingredients

1 cup finely diced carrots
1 cup sliced bananas
2 cups vanilla low-fat yogurt
1 cup coconut milk, unsweetened
1/4 cups shredded unsweetened coconut
14 teaspoons of cinnamon
1/4 teaspoons of fresh ginger
2 tablespoons of honey
1 cup of ice

Directions

1. In a blender, combine all of the ingredients and mix until smooth.
2. Pour into cold glasses and serve immediately.

Information on Nutrition

Sodium 196.3 mg,
potassium 467.0 mg,
total carbs 62.2 g,
dietary fiber 4.5 g,
sugars 48.5 g,
protein 11.4 g

The lime in the coconut smoothie serves as a garnish.

Ingredients

2 cups vanilla low-fat yogurt
1 cup coconut milk, unsweetened
1 teaspoon lime juice
12 cups unsweetened shredded coconut 1 teaspoon lime zest
1 teaspoon grated fresh ginger
2 teaspoons of honey (or sugar alternative of choice)
1 cup of ice

Directions

1. In a blender, combine all of the ingredients and mix until smooth.

2. Pour into a cold glass and serve immediately.

Information on Nutrition

Total fat: 14.5 g;
saturated fat: 13.0 g;
sodium: 160.1 mg; potassium: 29.8 mg; total carbs: 42.2 g;
dietary fiber: 2.0 g; sugars: 37.4 g; protein: 10.5 g.

Servings of Caribbean Love Smoothie

Ingredients

1/2 cups fresh pineapple,
chopped into pieces 2 cups mango,
diced 1 cup banana, sliced
1/2 cups vanilla low-fat yogurt
1/2 cups coconut milk, unsweetened
1 cup of ice

Directions

1. In a blender, combine all of the ingredients and mix until smooth.
2. Serve immediately in glasses that have been well cooled.

Information on Nutrition

Total fat 2.4 g,
saturated fat 1.8 g,
sodium 46.6 mg,

potassium 535.9 mg,
total carbohydrate 54.5 g,
dietary fiber 4.9 g,
sugars 42.4 g,
protein 4.1 g

Hoppin' Jalapeno Verde Smoothie 2
Serves 1

Ingredients

2 cups spinach,
fresh
1/2 cups orange juice
1 cup fresh pineapple, cubed;
1 teaspoon jalapeo pepper, diced
1 cup of ice

Directions

1. In a blender,
combine all of the ingredients and mix until smooth.
2. Serve immediately in glasses that have been well cooled.

Information on Nutrition

Sodium 25.2 mg,
potassium 388.3 mg,
total carbs 17.4 g,
dietary fiber 1.9 g,
sugars 13.9 g,
protein 1.8 g

Servings of Tropical Green Smoothie

Ingredients

2 cups spinach, fresh
1 cup cucumber, diced;
1 cup peaches;
1 cup mango;
1 cup fresh pineapple;
1 cup unsweetened coconut milk.
1 cup of ice

Directions

1. In a blender,
combine all of the ingredients and mix until smooth.
2. Serve immediately in glasses that have been well cooled.

Information on Nutrition

181.8 calories, 3.5 g
total fat, 2.6 g
saturated fat,
41.9 mg sodium,
646.0 mg potassium,
39.1 g total carbs,
5.2 g dietary fiber,
31.2 g sugars,
3.0 g protein

Vitamin C Power Drink

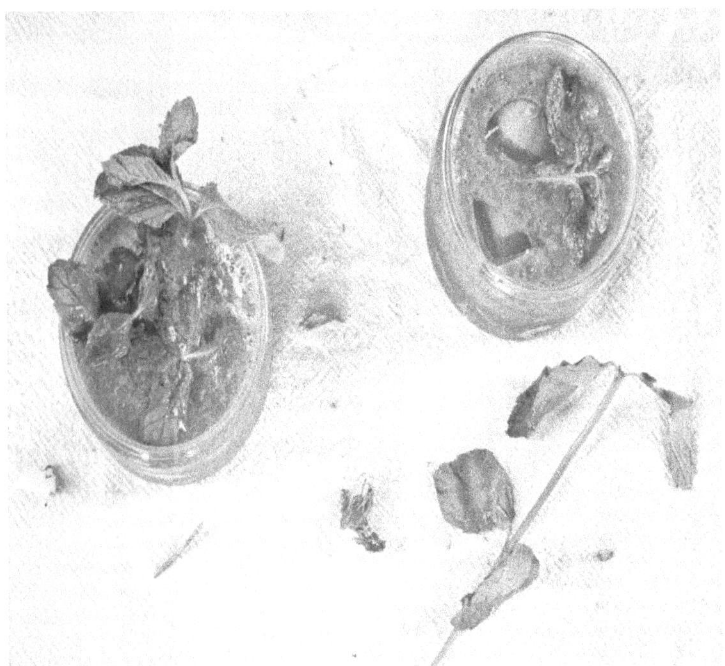

Serves 2

Ingredients:

2 cups of orange segments
2 cups sliced carrots
1 cup diced Granny Smith apple
1 cup fresh raspberries
1/2 cup orange juice
1 cup of ice
Directions
1. In a blender, combine all of the ingredients and mix until smooth.
2. Serve immediately in glasses that have been well cooled.
Information on Nutrition
Total fat 0.8 g, saturated fat 0.1 g,

Cholesterol 0.0 mg, sodium 44.7 mg,
Potassium 801.1 mg,
Total carbs 48.2 g,

Dietary fiber 11.7 g, sugars 31.2 g,
 Protein 3.5 g

Peachy as a Pea Smoothie

Serves 2

Ingredients:
2 cups spinach, fresh
1/2 cup peas, frozen
2 cups diced mango

1 cup sliced bananas
1 teaspoon lime juice
1 cup coconut milk, unsweetened
1 cup of ice

Directions
1. In a blender, combine all of the ingredients and mix until smooth.
2. Pour into a cold glass and serve immediately.

Information on Nutrition
Sodium 83.4 mg,

Potassium 789.2 mg,

 Total carbs 56.3 g,

Dietary fiber 7.2 g,

Sugars 39.0 g, protein 5.0 g

Make a Plan Smoothie

Serves 2

Ingredients:
1 cup of chopped dates
1 cup vanilla low-fat yogurt
1 cup skim milk
1/2 teaspoon pure vanilla extract
2 teaspoons of honey (or sugar alternative of choice)
1/2 teaspoon ground nutmeg
1 cup of ice
Directions
1. In a blender, combine all of the ingredients and mix until smooth.
2. Serve immediately in glasses that have been well cooled.
Information on Nutrition
398.4 calories, 1.4 g total fat,

0.8 g saturated fat,

123.5 mg sodium,

 777.6 mg potassium,

92.2 g total carbs, 7.1 g dietary fiber,

81.4 g sugars, 10.8 g protein

Very savory
some mornings call for something with a bit more substance, or if beginning your day on a sweet note isn't your thing. These dishes combine high-quality proteins and fresh veggies to provide you with energy-boosting nourishment to start your day.

Black Bean Omelet

Serves 2

Ingredients:
1 tablespoon of olive oil
4 beaten eggs
1/4 cup chopped fresh cilantro
1/2 teaspoon black pepper
1/4 cup diced tomato

2 tablespoons diced red onion
1/2 cup cooked black beans (rinse completely if using canned)
1/2 tablespoon cumin
1/4 cup low-fat shredded Monterey Jack cheese

Directions

1. Heat the olive oil in an omelet pan or small sauté pan over medium heat.
2. Combine the eggs, cilantro, and black pepper in a mixing bowl.
3. Combine the tomato, red onion, black beans, and cumin in a separate dish.
4. Seep the egg mixture into the pan and cook, stirring gently around the edges with a spatula to enable more of the unset egg to seep out into the sides and below. Continue repeating this for around 3–4 minutes.
5. Flip the omelet over and top with the black bean mixture and cheese. Cook for a further 1-2 minutes after folding the omelet in half.
6. Remove the pan from the heat and serve immediately.

Information on Nutrition

Total fat 17.9 g,

Saturated fat 6.2 g,

Sodium 215.3 mg, potassium 422.0 mg,

Total carbs 15.2 g, dietary fiber 4.6 g,

Sugars 0.4 g, protein 19.7 g

Mediterranean Quiche

Serves 2

Ingredients:

1 whole wheat pie crust (homemade or store-bought)
1 tablespoon extra-virgin olive oil
1 cup chopped red onion
2 crushed and chopped garlic cloves
1 cup diced zucchini 1 cup sliced mushrooms
1/4 cup chopped spinach,

14 cups sundried tomatoes,

1/4 cup fresh basil,

4 eggs
1 cup skim milk
1/2 cup crumbled goat cheese

Directions

1. Preheat the oven to 375°F and line a 9-inch pie dish with pie crust.
2. Heat the olive oil in a large sauté pan over medium heat.
3. Combine the onion, garlic, and zucchini in a mixing bowl. Cook for 2 minutes.
4. Combine the mushrooms, spinach, sundried tomatoes, and basil in a mixing bowl.
Continue to sauté for another 2–3 minutes. Set aside after removing from the heat.
5. Combine the eggs and milk in a mixing bowl. Whisk until thoroughly combined.
6. Spread the veggie mixture evenly over the pie shell.
7. Add the egg mixture and top with the goat cheese.
8. Bake for 30 to 35 minutes, or until the quiche is set in the middle.
9. Remove from the oven and set aside for a few minutes before serving.

Information on Nutrition

303.5 calories,

17.7 g total fat, 8.2 g saturated fat,

320.6 mg sodium, 374.0 mg potassium,

19.8 g total carbs, 4.1 g dietary fiber,

5.3 g sugars, 11.7 g protein

Frittata with Tomatoes and Zucchini

Serves 2

Ingredients:
1 tablespoon vegetable oil

1/4 cup chopped shallots
2 cups sliced zucchini
1 teaspoon dried oregano
1 teaspoon fresh thyme
1 teaspoon ground black pepper
8 eggs
1/4 cup skim milk
1 cup shredded low-fat mild cheddar cheese

1 cup sliced tomatoes

Directions

1. Heat the oven to 425°F.
2. Heat the vegetable oil in an oven-safe skillet over medium heat.
3. Combine the shallots and zucchini in a mixing bowl. Cook for 5 minutes, or until the vegetables are soft. Oregano, thyme, and black pepper to taste.
4. Combine the eggs and milk in a mixing bowl. To combine, whisk everything together. Stir in the cheese.
5. Leak the egg mixture into the skillet and cook for 10–12 minutes, raising the edges with a spatula periodically to enable some of the liquid egg to leak out into the sides and below.
6. Arrange the tomato slices on top and bake the pan.
7. Bake for 15-20 minutes, or until the middle is set.
8. Set aside to cool slightly before serving.

Information on Nutrition

Sodium 219.3 mg,

Potassium 355.4 mg,

Total carbohydrate 6.0 g, dietary fiber 1.2 g,

Sugars 1.8 g,

Protein 14.1 g

Mini Egg Cups with Mushrooms and Herbed Goat Cheese

Serves 2

Ingredients:

1 tablespoon extra-virgin olive oil
1/2 cup chopped yellow onion
2 cups chopped portabella mushrooms
1 tablespoon chopped fresh chives
1 teaspoon fresh thyme
1/2 tsp black pepper
1/2 cup crumbled goat cheese
8 eggs
3 tablespoons skim milk

Cooking spray or olive oil
Directions
1. Preheat the oven to 350°F and grease 12 muffin cups.
2. Heat the olive oil in a sauté pan over medium heat.
3. Cook for 2 minutes, or until the onion is barely soft.
Combine the mushrooms, chives, thyme, and black pepper
in a mixing bowl. Cook, stirring constantly, for another 2-3
minutes, or until the mushrooms are soft.
4. Combine the eggs and milk in a mixing basin. To
combine, whisk everything together well.
5. Divide the mushroom mixture evenly among the muffin
cups. Then top with the crumbled goat cheese and the egg
mixture.
6. Place in the oven and bake for 15 minutes, or until the
center is set.
7. Set aside to cool somewhat before serving.
Information on Nutrition
180.2 calories,

12.7 g total fat,

5.2 g saturated fat, 169.8 mg sodium,

207.0 mg potassium, 3.1 g total carbs,

0.5 g dietary fiber, 1.4 g sugars,

13.1 g protein

Fiery Baked Eggs

Serves 2

Ingredients:
1 tablespoon extra-virgin olive oil
2 crushed and chopped garlic cloves
1/2 teaspoon red pepper flakes, crushed
2 cups chopped tomatoes
2 cups chopped fresh spinach
1 diced jalapeno pepper
1 cup tomato or vegetable juice (low sodium)
1/4 cup fresh grated Parmesan cheese
If preferred, whole wheat bread may be served.
Directions

1. Heat the olive oil in a skillet over medium heat.
2. Combine the garlic, jalapeño, and crushed red pepper flakes in a mixing bowl. Sauté until aromatic, about 1-2 minutes.
3. Combine the tomatoes and spinach in a mixing bowl. Cook for 2-3 minutes. Cook until the liquid starts to boil, then add the tomato juice.
4. Scatter the eggs on top and top with Parmesan cheese. Cook for 5-7 minutes, or until the eggs are done to your liking.
5. If wanted, serve warm with whole wheat bread for dipping.

Information on Nutrition

Sodium 123.1 mg,

Potassium 914.2 mg,

Total carbs 15.0 g,

Dietary fiber 3.1 g, sugars 4.7 g,

Protein 9.6 g

Sweet Potato Breakfast Bake

Serves 6-8

Ingredients

8 oz. ground turkey,

2 tsp. olive oil
4 cups shredded sweet potato
1 cup chopped yellow onion
2 cups chopped spinach
1 cup shredded low-fat cheddar cheese
2 cups cottage cheese (low fat)
8 beaten eggs
1 tablespoon sage

1 teaspoon fresh thyme
1 teaspoon ground black pepper
Directions
1. Preheat the oven to 375°F and lightly butter a 9x13 baking dish.
2. In a pan, brown the turkey for about 5-7 minutes over medium heat.
3. Toss the sweet potatoes, onion, and olive oil together. Spread the mixture in the bottom of the baking dish.
4. Combine the cheddar cheese, cottage cheese, eggs, sage, thyme, and black pepper in a separate dish. Pour over the sweet potatoes and mix thoroughly.
5. Bake in the oven for 50–55 minutes, or until the middle is set.
6. Set aside to cool somewhat before serving.
Information on Nutrition
Sodium 317.4 mg,

Potassium 295.9 mg,

Total carbs 21.0 g, dietary fiber 2.5 g,

Sugars 1.7 g,

Protein 24.3 g

Breakfast Nachos

Serves 4

Ingredients

1 tablespoon of olive oil
4 beaten eggs
14 cups chopped cilantro
1/2 tsp cayenne pepper
1 cup cooked pinto beans (rinse thoroughly if using canned)
1/2 teaspoon chili powder
1 cup chopped tomatoes
1/2 cup chopped red bell pepper
1 sliced avocado

1/2 cup reduced-fat cheddar cheese
1 cup chopped green onion

1/4 cup low-fat plain yogurt
4 cups of blue corn tortilla chips without salt were added.
Directions
1. Heat the oven to 200°F. Place the tortilla chips on a baking sheet and reheat in the oven while you prepare the remainder of the dinner.
2. In a small saucepan over medium-low heat, cook the pinto beans and chili powder.
3. Melt the butter in a pan over medium heat. Add the eggs, cilantro, and cayenne pepper to the skillet and mix well. Cook, scrambling, until the eggs are soft-set or done to your liking. Take the pan off the heat.
4. Arrange the reheated chips on a dish and top with the beans, eggs, tomatoes, red bell pepper, avocado, low-fat cheddar cheese, green onion, and plain yogurt.
5. Serve right away.
Information on Nutrition
Sodium 277.7 mg,

Potassium 672.4 mg,

Total carbohydrate 61.7 g,

Dietary fiber 13.5 g,

Sugars 2.2 g,

Protein 21.5 g

Huevos Rancheros with Avocado Salsa

Serves 4

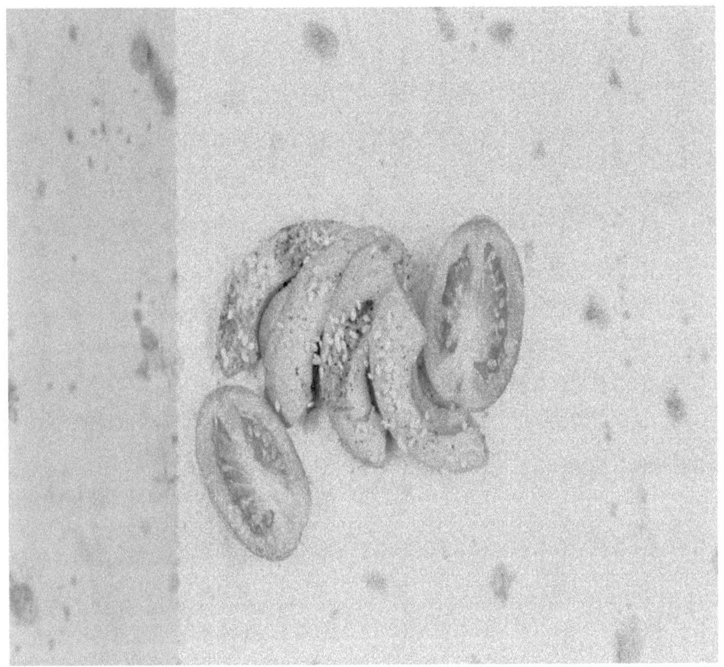

Ingredients
2 cups cooked black beans (rinse well if using canned)
2 tbsp. olive oil
2 minced garlic cloves
2 cups spinach, fresh
1 tsp. chili powder
1 tsp. lime juice
4 eggs
1/4 cup cilantro, fresh
1/4 cup diced radishes
4 warmed whole wheat tortillas

Salsa de Avocado
1 chopped avocado

1 cup diced tomatoes

1/2 cup diced red onion
1 tablespoon chopped jalapeo pepper
1 teaspoon cayenne pepper sauce
1/2 tablespoon cumin
1 tsp. lime juice

Directions
1. Toss all of the ingredients for the avocado salsa together. Put aside, cover, and put away.
2. Heat the olive oil in a large pot or skillet over medium heat. Sauté the garlic and spinach for 2 minutes.
3. Combine the black beans, chili powder, and lime juice in a mixing bowl. Cook for 3 minutes, mashing gently. Reduce the heat to k be and keep warm until ready to use.
4. Cook the eggs as desired. (e.g., scrambled, poached)
5. Spoon the bean mixture onto each tortilla. Top with avocado salsa, followed by the egg. Garnish with radishes and fresh cilantro.
6. Serve right away.

Information on Nutrition
Sodium 301.8 mg,

 Potassium 810.0 mg,

Total carbs 51.0 g,

Dietary fiber 14.6 g,

Sugars 2.4 g, protein 19.8 g

<u>**Breakfast Pizza with Asparagus and Eggs on Flatbread**</u>

Serves 2

Ingredients
1 tbsp olive oil (divided)
2 garlic cloves, minced

1/4 cup shallots, diced

2 cups asparagus spears, chopped

1 cup mushrooms, sliced
1/2 c. goat cheese
1/2 teaspoon dried oregano
1/2 teaspoon fresh thyme
1/2 teaspoon black pepper

1 whole wheat flatbread (large) (or 2 smaller pieces)
1/4 cup low-fat milk 3 eggs
1/4 cup chopped fresh chives

Directions

1. Heat the oven to 350°F.
2. Place the flatbread on a baking pan and brush with olive oil.
3. In a pan, heat the remaining olive oil and add the garlic and onions. Cook until aromatic, about 1-2 minutes.
4. Finally, add the asparagus and mushrooms. Cook for 3–4 minutes, or until the vegetables are soft.
5. Combine the goat cheese, oregano, and thyme in a mixing bowl and distribute equally over the flatbread or sprinkle in little spoonfuls around the top.
6. Arrange the asparagus mixture and tomatoes on top.
7. Bake for 10–15 minutes in a preheated oven.
Meanwhile, in the previously used skillet, whisk together the eggs, milk, and chives. Scramble while cooking until soft set or doneness is desired.
9. Take the flatbread out of the oven and top with the eggs.
10. Serve right away.

Information on Nutrition

Sodium 409.8 mg,

Potassium 887.9 mg,

Total carbs 24.4 g, dietary fiber 8.7 g,

Sugars 2.9 g,

Protein 28.1 g

Spinach and Carrot Hash Browns

Serves 4

Ingredients
1 tablespoon extra-virgin olive oil
2 cups peeled and shredded sweet potatoes
2 cups shredded carrots
2 cups chopped spinach
2 crushed and chopped garlic cloves
1/2 teaspoon ground nutmeg
1/2 teaspoon fresh thyme
1 paprika teaspoon
1 beaten egg Scallions, cut for garnish
For garnish, use plain low-fat yogurt.

Directions
1. Place the sweet potatoes and carrots in a sieve and
squeeze out as much liquid as possible before transferring

to a dish.
2. Combine the sweet potatoes, carrots, spinach, garlic, nutmeg, thyme, paprika, and egg in a large mixing bowl. Combine thoroughly.
3. In a large pan over medium-high heat, heat the olive oil.
4. Press the hash brown mixture into the skillet's bottom and heat for 5 minutes, or until the bottom starts to crisp. Toss with a spatula gently before turning so that the majority of the uncooked side is now contacting the heat.
5. Cook for another 5–7 minutes, or until desired crispness is achieved.
6. Garnish with scallions and plain yogurt before serving.
Information on Nutrition
143.7 calories,

4.9 g total fat,

 0.9 g saturated fat,

76.1 mg sodium, 412.4 mg potassium,

22.0 g total carbs,

3.9 g dietary fiber,

 2.6 g sugars, 3.6 g protein

Grab and Go
are you seeking the ultimate healthy meal that you can consume quickly in your few precious spare minutes in the morning, or something that you can grab and go? Try one of these simple, DASH-friendly breakfast ideas.

Oatmeal Power Bars

Serves 4

Ingredients

2 bananas, mashed until smooth.
1 teaspoon vanilla essence, pure
2 c. oatmeal
1/2 cup chopped walnuts

1/4 cup crushed flax meal
1/4 cup chopped dates
1/2 teaspoon ground cinnamon
1/2 teaspoon ground nutmeg
Directions

1. Preheat the oven to 350°F and gently grease an 8-by-8 baking dish.
2. Combine the banana and vanilla essence in a mixing bowl. Blend well.
3. Combine the oats, walnuts, flax meal, dates, cinnamon, and nutmeg in a mixing bowl. Combine thoroughly.
4. Place the baking dish in the oven and pat the mixture into the bottom. 35–40 minutes, or until the edges are faintly browned.
5. Allow to cool somewhat before cutting into bars.

Information on Nutrition

Sodium 1.4 mg,

Potassium 375.5 mg,

Total carbs 43.1 g,

Dietary fiber 6.9 g, sugars 14.8 g,

Protein 6.6 g

<u>Nutty Chai Breakfast Bombs</u>

Serves 6

Ingredients
1/2 cup unsalted almonds 1 cup unsalted walnuts
1/2 cup sunflower seeds, unsalted
1 cup shredded unsweetened coconut
1/2 cup chopped dried apricots
2 tbsp. honey (or sugar alternative of choice)
1/4 cup applesauce, unsweetened
1/4 cup flax meal, ground
2 teaspoons grated fresh ginger
1 teaspoon ground cinnamon
1/2 teaspoon ground nutmeg
1/2 teaspoon ground cardamom

3 tbsp sugar-free peanut butter
Directions
1. Line 12 muffin cups with paper liners and set aside.
2. In a food mill or food processor, combine the walnuts, almonds, and sunflower seeds. Transfer to a basin after blending until a coarse meal is created.
3. Combine the coconut, apricots, honey, applesauce, flax meal, ginger, cinnamon, nutmeg, cardamom, and peanut butter in a large mixing bowl. Mix well.
4. Divide the mixture evenly among the muffin cups and push down firmly.
5. Place the muffin pans in the freezer for 45 minutes, or until solid.
6. Serve immediately or keep in the refrigerator until ready to use.
Information on Nutrition
Total fat 36.3 g,

Saturated fat 9.2 g,

Sodium 43.1 mg, potassium 413.6 mg,

Total carbs 26.7 g, dietary fiber 7.7 g,

Sugars 15.2 g, protein 11.2 g

Super Energy Breakfast Bars

Serves 12

Ingredients
2 cups oatmeal (distributed)
1/4 cup flax meal 12 cups chia seeds
1/2 cup walnuts, unsalted
1 cup almonds, unsalted
1 teaspoon ground cinnamon
2 cups mashed bananas
1/4 cup nut butter
1 teaspoon of coconut oil
1/4 cup honey (or desired substitution)
a teaspoon of vanilla extract

1/2 cup pumpkin seeds, unsalted
1 cup fresh blueberries
1/2 cup fresh pineapple, cut
1/4 cup coconut milk, unsweetened
1/2 cup low-fat cream cheese, cut into cubes
Directions
1. Preheat the oven to 350°F and gently grease a 9-by-9 baking dish.
2. In a food processor, combine the oats, chia seeds, flax meal, walnuts, almonds, and cinnamon and pulse until a coarse meal forms.
3. Combine the bananas, cashew butter, coconut oil, honey, and vanilla essence in a mixing dish. Blend well.
4. Combine and thoroughly mix the wet and dry ingredients. Place the baking dish in the oven and spread the batter evenly. Bake for 10–15 minutes, or until the top is brown.
5. Meanwhile, in a mixing dish, add the pumpkin seeds, blueberries, pineapple, coconut milk, and cream cheese. Toss to combine.
6. Take the crust out of the oven and immediately put the topping on top. Return the pan to the oven and bake for another 20 minutes.
7. Allow to cool somewhat before slicing.
Information on Nutrition
Total fat: 15.0 g,

Cholesterol: 3.7 mg,

Sodium: 22.8 mg, potassium: 300.8 mg,

Total carbs: 31.7 g,

Dietary fiber: 5.9 g,

Sugars: 11.7 g, protein: 7.7 g

Muesli Snack Mix

Serves 8

Ingredients
5 cup oats, rolled
1/4 cup unsalted sunflower seeds 1 cup chopped walnuts
1/4 cup pumpkin seeds, unsalted
1/2 cup toasted wheat germ
1 cup dried raisins
1 cup dried cranberries
1/4 cup brown sugar or sugar substitute

Directions
1. Whisk together all of the ingredients.
2. Place in an airtight container to store.

Information on Nutrition
Sodium 5.5 mg,

Potassium 343.3 mg,

 Total carbs 74.2 g,

 Dietary fiber 9.0 g,

Sugars 28.9 g, protein 12.3 g

Amazing Protein Loaf

Serves 12

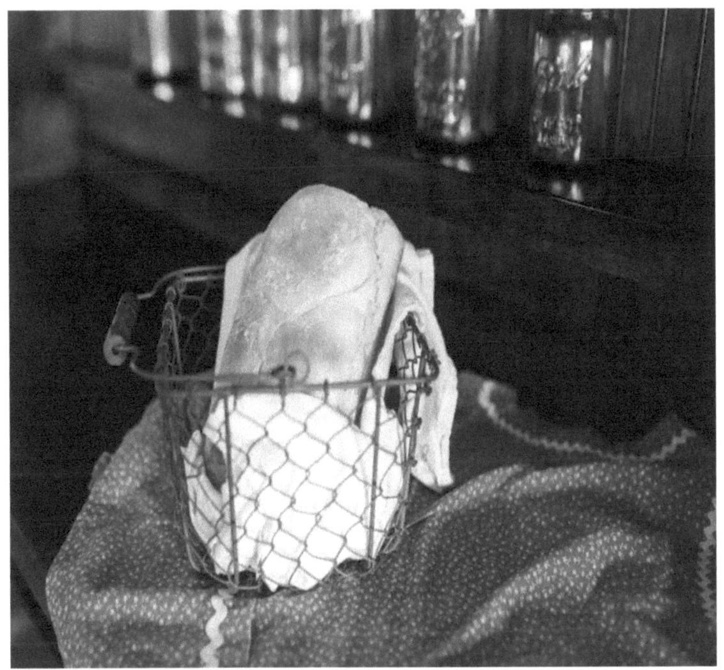

Ingredients

1/2 cup whole wheat flour

1/2 cup ground oats

1/4 cup ground flax meal
2 1/2 teaspoons baking powder
1/2 teaspoon ground allspice
1/2 teaspoon ground cinnamon
1 cup of chopped dates
1 cup warm water
1 cup blueberries, dry
1/2 cup chopped apple
8 beaten egg whites

1/4 cup vanilla low-fat yogurt
1/4 cup applesauce, unsweetened
1 cup chopped walnuts

Directions

1. Heat the oven to 350°F and gently grease a loaf pan.
2. Combine the dates and boiling water in a mixing bowl. Allow yourself to sit for at least 10 minutes.
3. Combine the whole wheat flour, oats, flax meal, baking powder, allspice, and cinnamon in a mixing bowl. Combine thoroughly.
4. Combine the soaked dates, blueberries, apple, egg whites, yogurt, applesauce, and walnuts in a separate dish. Combine thoroughly.
5. Mix the dry components into the wet ingredients until just combined.
6. Pour the batter into the loaf pan and bake for 30 minutes.
7. Bake for 45 minutes, or until a toothpick inserted into the middle comes out clean.
8. Remove from the pan and let it stand aside to cool somewhat.

Information on Nutrition

Sodium 121.9 mg,

Potassium 171.0 mg, total carbs 41.5 g,

Dietary fiber 5.7 g,

Sugars 20.5 g,

Protein 7.5 g

Whole grain toast with fruited ricotta spread

Serves 4

Ingredients
4 toasted slices of whole grain bread
1 cup ricotta cheese (low fat)
1 teaspoon orange zest

2 tablespoons of honey (or sugar alternative of choice)
1 tablespoon minced fresh mint

1/2 cup peaches, neatly diced

1/4 cup almonds, sliced
Optional additional fresh fruit for garnish
Directions
1. Combine the ricotta cheese, orange zest, honey, mint,

and peaches in a mixing bowl. Blend well.
2. Spread equally over each piece of whole wheat bread and garnish with sliced almonds and fresh fruit, if preferred.

Information on Nutrition
Sodium 187.0 mg,

Potassium 162.0 mg,

Total carbs 20.0 g,

Dietary fiber 3.2 g, sugars 5.5 g,

Protein 12.4 g

Cinnamon Walnut Breakfast Parfait

Serves 2

Ingredients
1 cup vanilla low-fat yogurt
1 tsp. chia seeds
1/2 cup chopped walnuts

1 cup Granny Smith apples
1 tablespoon of honey
1/4 teaspoon ground cinnamon
Directions
1. Combine the yogurt and chia seeds in a mixing bowl.
Place aside.
2. Combine the apples, walnuts, honey, and cinnamon in a

separate bowl. Combine thoroughly.

3. Alternate layers of apple-walnut mixture and yogurt in two separate serving glasses until all ingredients are utilized.

4. Serve immediately or refrigerate until ready to serve.

Information on Nutrition

Sodium 70.8 mg,

Potassium 207.0 mg,

Total carbs 34.6 g,

Dietary fiber 6.0 g

Sugars 26.1 g, protein 10.7 g

PB&J Parfait

Serves 2

Ingredients

1 cup vanilla low-fat yogurt
1 cup unsweetened peanut butter
1 cup fresh blueberries
1/2 cup chopped almonds
1 tablespoon of honey
1/2 teaspoon ground cinnamon

Directions

1. Combine the yogurt and peanut butter in a mixing bowl.
Set aside after mixing until smooth.
2. Combine the blueberries, almonds, honey, and cinnamon
in a mixing bowl. Toss to combine.
3. Alternate layers of yogurt and blueberry mixture in two

separate serving glasses until all ingredients are utilized.
4. Serve right away or refrigerate until ready to use.
Information on Nutrition
Sodium 112.1 mg,

Potassium 67.3 mg,

 Total carbs 31.1 g,

 Dietary fiber 2.5 g,

Sugars 27.1 g,

Protein 6.8 g

Breakfast Pops with Granola

4-6 servings (depending on mold size)

Ingredients
2 cups vanilla low-fat yogurt
1/2 cup strawberries, diced

1/2 cup fresh pineapple, diced

1/2 cup mango, diced

1/4 cup sugar-free granola
Directions
1. In a mixing bowl, combine the yogurt, strawberries,

pineapple, and mango. Combine thoroughly.
2. Spoon the yogurt mixture into the ice pop molds and top
with a sprinkling of oats.
3. Freeze for several hours or overnight in the freezer.

Information on Nutrition

Total fat 1.4 g, saturated fat 0.8 g, sodium 77.0 mg,
potassium 117.2 mg, total carbs 25.5 g, dietary fiber 1.7 g,
sugars 22.0 g, protein 5.1 g

Fruit Quesadilla

Serves 4

Ingredients

1 cup sliced strawberries

1/2 cup mango

2 cups chopped apricots

2 teaspoons of orange juice
1/2 cup low-fat ricotta cheese 1 tablespoon fresh mint,
chopped
1 teaspoon lime zest

1/2 teaspoon pure vanilla essence

1/4 cup chopped walnuts
4 whole grain tortillas
Directions
1. In a saucepan, combine the strawberries, mango, apricots, orange juice, and mint. Heat over medium-low heat until the fruit softens and releases juices, about 5–7 minutes.
2. Combine the ricotta cheese, lime zest, vanilla essence, and walnuts in a mixing dish. Combine thoroughly.
3. Divide the cheese mixture among the tortillas.
4. Melt the tortilla in a pan over medium heat. Fold in half and add part of the fruit filling.
5. Cook for 1-2 minutes on each side. Repeat with the remaining tortillas.
6. Serve hot.

Information on Nutrition
Total fat 11.0 g,

Saturated fat 3.0 g,

Sodium 320.3 mg,

Potassium 395.2 mg, total carbohydrate 40.7 g,

Dietary fiber 6.4 g,

Sugars 15.6 g, protein 10.2 g

Italian Breakfast Burritos

Serves 4

Ingredients
1 cup cooked cannellini beans (rinse well if using canned)
1 tablespoon extra-virgin olive oil
2 crushed and chopped garlic cloves
1/2 cup red onion, diced

1/2 cup red bell pepper, chopped

2 cups fresh spinach, torn

1 cup tomato, diced

1/2 cup artichoke hearts, chopped
6 beaten eggs

1/2 teaspoon oregano
12 tsp black pepper
12 cups low-fat mozzarella cheese
14 cups torn fresh basil
4 big whole wheat burrito tortillas
Directions
1. Heat the beans in a small saucepan over low heat. Warm up until ready to use.
2. Heat the olive oil in a skillet over medium heat. Cook until the garlic and crushed red pepper flakes are aromatic, about 1 minute.
3. Stir in the red pepper and onion. Before adding the spinach, tomatoes, and artichoke hearts, sauté for 1–2 minutes. Cook for another 2–3 minutes.
4. Arrange the tortillas on a plate and spread each with pesto.
5. Add the bean and veggie mixture over top.
6. Add the eggs, oregano, and black pepper to the same pan where you cooked the veggies. Cook while scrambling the eggs until they are softly set. When finished, transfer to the burritos.
7. Garnish with fresh basil and mozzarella cheese. Each tortilla should be carefully rolled.
8. Serve hot.
Information on Nutrition
Sodium 406.2 mg,

Potassium 626.5 mg,

 Total carbs 41.2 g,

Dietary fiber 7.4 g, sugars 2.9 g,

Protein 19.3 g

Breakfast Sliders

Serves 4

Ingredients
1 tablespoon extra-virgin olive oil
4 thick tomato slices
1/4 teaspoon black pepper
1 cup spinach, fresh
1/2 cup arugula

1/4 cup chopped fresh basil
a teaspoon balsamic vinegar
4 beaten eggs

2 tbsp. fat-free milk
1/4 cup goat cheese

1 tablespoon chopped fresh chives
4 whole wheat English muffins, halved and toasted
Directions
1. Combine the spinach, arugula, basil, and balsamic
vinegar in a mixing dish. Set aside after tossing to combine.
2. Melt the butter in a pan over medium-high heat.
3. Cook the tomato slices for 1–2 minutes on each side.
Set aside after removing from the pan. Reduce the heat to
medium in the skillet.
4. Combine the eggs, milk, and chives in a mixing bowl
and pour into the skillet.
Cook the eggs in a scrambled state until they are softly set.
5. Top each English muffin with a thin coating of goat
cheese.
6. Place the greens mixture, a tomato slice, and an egg on
one side of the muffin.
7. Serve immediately with the second half of the English
muffin.
Information on Nutrition
Sodium 556.3 mg,

Potassium 316.8 mg,

Total carbs 29.0 g,

Dietary fiber 4.9 g,

Sugars 0.7 g,

Protein 15.4 g

Conclusion

when it comes to how we like to start our mornings, we all have various tastes and preferences. For some of us, it's the ideal cup of coffee and a simple bowl of fruit and yogurt, while for others, the day doesn't begin until a warm, high-protein meal is swallowed with pleasure. Whatever your style, there is a DASH choice for you, and you may discover just what you need inside the pages of this book. Each breakfast is crafted with the healthiest and freshest ingredients to get your day off to the best possible start. You are well on your way to attaining your health objectives with the dietary plan that has been ranked among the best in the world for five years in a row, along with the morning recipes featured in this book. Allow the DASH diet's pure simplicity to assist you in becoming a healthier, happier person.

Printed by Libri Plureos GmbH in Hamburg,
Germany